AF573615

OTHER HELEN EXLEY GIFTBOOKS IN THIS SERIES:

Over 30s' Jokes
A Spread of Over 40s' Jokes
A Jubilee of Over 60s' Jokes
Over 70s' Jokes
Old Wrecks' Jokes
A Round of Golf Jokes
A Chuckle of Kids' Jokes
A Romp of Naughty Jokes

Published in 1994 by Helen Exley Giftbooks in Great Britain.
Selection and arrangement copyright © Helen Exley Creative 2016
Cartoons copyright © Bill Stott 1994
The moral rights of the authors have been asserted.

12 11 10 9 8 7 6 5

Cartoons by Bill Stott.
Edited by Elizabeth Cotton.
Series Editor: Helen Exley.

ISBN: 978-1-84634-225-7

A copy of the CIP data is available from the British Library on request. All rights reserved. No part of this publication may be reproduced or transmitted in any form or by any means, electronic or mechanical, including photocopy, recording or any information storage and retrieval system without permission in writing from the publisher.
Printed in China.

Acknowledgemets: The publishers gratefully acknowledge permission to reprint copyright material. They would be pleased to hear from any copyright holders not here acknowledged. Extracts from *Middle Age Rage and other Male Indignities* COPYRIGHT © 1987 by Fred Shoenberg reprinted by permission of Simon & Schuster, Inc. **IMPORTANT COPYRIGHT NOTICE:** PAM BROWN, PETER GRAY, MIKE KNOWLES © HELEN EXLEY 1994.

Helen Exley Giftbooks, 16 Chalk Hill, Watford, Herts WD19 4BG, UK.
www.helenexleygiftbooks.com

A TRIUMPH OF OVER 50s' JOKES

CARTOONS BY BILL STOTT

HELEN EXLEY®

You're Never Too Old

"Fifty is the time to get up and go – before everything else does."

PAM BROWN

*

"You're never too old to become younger."

MAE WEST

*

"It is better to wear out than rust out."

RICHARD CUMBERLAND

*

"You can't turn back the clock. But you can wind it up again."

BONNIE PRUDDEN

*

"WELL.... YOU'RE ONLY 50 ONCE - RIGHT?"

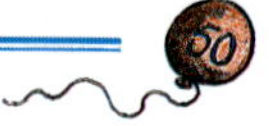

The Symptoms

"When you are old your body creaks and your knees knock and your teeth fall out."

ADRIAN TYDD, AGE 10

"HONEY - COME QUICK - I'VE FOUND A BROWN HAIR!"

"I'M THE SAME WEIGHT AS WHEN I WAS 25. UNFORTUNATELY, AT 50 AT LEAST 30% OF IT'S IN ONE PLACE..."

"At middle age you suddenly become appalled by the way that modern mirrors distort the reflection."

PETER GRAY

*

"The disadvantage of being old is not looking as nice as you did when you were young. It is like looking in a before and after picture but the other way around."

GINO MIELE

*

"Just think, if only you could snap your fingers on the birthday you wanted and never grow any older! HUH! Birthdays won't even let you do that because you've got that much artheritis your fingers won't snap."

SUSAN CURZON, AGE 12

*

"Are you going to have candles on your birthday cake?"

"No, it's a birthday party, not a torchlight procession."

CINDY PATTERSON

*

"When you have a birthday and you are middle aged your friends all clink their glasses and cheer and it gives you a headache."

PHILIP BROOKE, AGE 8

*

"You know you've had one birthday too many when your cake collapses from the weight of the candles."

P.D.F.

*

"Take my advice - it's best to ignore your birthday - unless you want it to grow old and rusty."

ESTHER REES

*

You're Definitely Over 50...

"... when your toenails are further off than they used to be."

*

"DON'T GET ME WRONG - A MOUNTAIN BIKE AT 50'S GREAT - PERSONALLY THOUGH - I'D LOSE THE LYCRA PANTS..."

"... when comfort triumphs at last over fashion."

PAM BROWN

*

"...when you need to have a rest after tying your shoelaces."

"...when keeping your hair on means wearing a toupee."

"...when you daren't stop on a busy high street in case some do-gooder wants to help you across the road."

MIKE KNOWLES

*

"... when your clothes no longer fit, and it's you who need the alterations."

EARL WILSON

*

When It Comes To Age, Keep Them Guessing!

"Fifty is the time between Well-preserved and Smart. Hang on to Elegance."

PAM BROWN

*

"If you want to stay young-looking, pick your parents very carefully."

DICK CLARK

*

"Nature gives you the face you have at twenty, but it's up to you to merit the face you have at fifty."

COCO CHANEL

*

"No woman should ever be quite accurate about her age. It looks so calculating."

OSCAR WILDE

*

"As long as a woman can look ten years younger than her own daughter, she is perfectly satisfied."

OSCAR WILDE

"WE'VE KICKED BOOZE AND SMOKING
AND HERE WE ARE - DOING
THINGS TOGETHER AGAIN..."

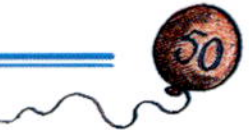

"After thirty-five years of marriage Sam's wife died. At the end of a proper mourning period, Sam looked at himself and said, 'Life is not over. I can go out and have some fun and perhaps meet a nice, younger woman and – who knows what?' Over an eighteen-month period Sam joined a gym to tone up, lost forty pounds, bought a toupee, had all his teeth capped, got a nose job, had a little tuck taken in his chin, grew a mustache, got contact lenses and bought a new youth-oriented wardrobe with elevator shoes. Finally one day he was ready to step out – he loved what he saw in the mirror. Unfortunately, that night Sam died and went to heaven, whereupon he met God. 'God,' said Sam, 'I was a kind and loving husband, a wonderful father and grandfather, a charitable person, and honest and hardworking in my business. I was just about to start a new life. Why did you do this?' 'Sam,' replied God, 'to tell you the truth, I didn't recognize you.'"

FRED SHOENBERG,
from *Middle Age Rage and other Male Indignities*

*

You Can't Believe A Woman...

"One should never trust a woman who tells one her real age. A woman who would tell anything."

OSCAR WILDE

"WE MELTED ALL YOUR CANDLES INTO ONE - THAT WAY WE GOT 50 ON ONE CAKE!"

"I refuse to admit that I am more than fifty-two, even if that does make my sons illegitimate."

NANCY ASTOR

*

"From birth to age 18, a girl needs good parents, from 18 to 35 she needs good looks, from 35 to 55 she needs a good personality, and from 55 on she needs cash."

SOPHIE TUCKER

*

"THERE'S NO NEED TO BREATHE IN THAT MUCH DADDY..."

WARNING SIGNS

"...you start to say things like 'In my day.'"

"...you get white hairs from worrying about your wrinkles."

"...you cling to the fact that Grandma Moses was older than you when she got going."

"... there are hills where none used to be."

"... your beautician, your hairdresser
and your dentist all stroke their heads
and sigh."

"... the doctor says 'You're very fit.' – But looks astonished."

PAM BROWN

*

"HE WAS A BEAUTIFUL CHILD...UNFORTUNATELY HE

PEAKED AT TWELVE..."

DOWNHILL ALL THE WAY…

“I’m at an age where my back goes out more than I do.”

PHYLLIS DILLER

*

“You know you’re getting older when you wake up with that morning after feeling and you didn’t do anything the night before.”

S.L.P.

*

“Old age is when candlelit dinners are no longer romantic because you can’t read the menu.”

CINDY PATTERSON

*

“The only two things we do with greater frequency in middle age are urinate and attend funerals.”

FRED SHOENBERG,
from *Middle Age Rage and other Male Indignities*

An Outbreak Of Wrinkles

"I wouldn't say my face was getting more wrinkled, but the other day it took a bead of sweat two hours to reach my chin."

"He was over 50 and he looked it. In fact his face was that hard and wrinkled the neighbours sharpened their knives on it."

"I wouldn't say her face was showing its age, but last week she was followed home by a group of archeologists."

"I wouldn't say she was wrinkled, but last year she went on holiday to India. And when she was sunbathing next to this river one of the local women used her face as a washboard."

MIKE KNOWLES

*

"DO YOU REALIZE THAT YOU AND I TOGETHER ARE OLDER THAN MOST OF THE STUFF YOU'RE LOOKING AT?"

You're A Piece Of Ancient History

"You know you must be pretty ancient when your grandchildren ask you for your personal recollections of Queen Victoria and life before electricity."

PETER DUGDALE

"HI – GRANDAD...."

"CALL ME GRANDMA ONE MORE TIME AND THINGS WILL GET REAL UGLY!"

"The denunciation of the young is a necessary part of the hygiene of older people, and greatly assists the circulation of the blood."

LOGAN PEARSALL SMITH

*

"Children are a great comfort in your old age – and they help you to reach it faster, too."

LIONEL M. KAUFFMAN

*

Bald Is Beautiful!

"In mathematical terms old age is a condition reached when the rate of your receding hairline is directly proportional to the expansion of your waist."

ANGUS WALKER

*

"Look on the brighter side of being bald. At least you don't have to wash your hair any more."

DARA O'CONNELL

*

"Remember the Teddy Boys? They used to dab a jar of Brylcreem on their hair and spend hours getting the quiff just right. Now it's a quick rub with some floor polish and they're off."

MIKE KNOWLES

*

WHO WANTS TO LIVE FOREVER?

"Life's a tough proposition but the first hundred years are the hardest."

WILSON MIZNER

*

"Life would be infinitely happier if we could only be born at the age of eighty and gradually approach eighteen."

MARK TWAIN

*

"Youth is a disease from which we all recover."

DOROTHY FULDHEIM

*

"I'll tell ya how to stay young: Hang around with older people."

BOB HOPE

*

"You're not as young as you used to be.
But you're not as old as you're going to be.
So watch it!"

IRISH TOAST

*

"The years that a woman subtracts from her age are not lost. They are added to other women's."

DIANE DE POITIERS

*

"WHAT DO YOU MEAN

– I LOOK YOUNGER THAN CAROL O'BRIEN?

CAROL O'BRIEN IS 56!"

"When women pass thirty, they first forget their age; when forty, they forget that they ever remembered it."

NINON DE LENCLOS

*

"My wife never lies about her age. She just tells everyone she's as old as I am. Then she lies about my age."

J.K.N.

*

"Man is old when he begins to hide his age; woman, when she begins to tell hers."

OSCAR WILDE

*

"I was born in 1962, true. And the room next to me was 1963."

JOAN RIVERS

*

"My husband never chases another woman. He's too fine, too decent, too old!"

GRACIE ALLEN

*

"At 50 you still get 'the urge' but can't remember what for..."

ANON

*

Have Heart, You're Not As Old As You Look

"Fifty is when friends of fifty haven't changed one bit – but all the forty-year-olds are getting to look a bit long in the tooth."

PAM BROWN

*

"Age – you just wake up one morning, and you got it."

MOMS MABLEY

*

"How come at a class reunion you feel so much younger than everybody else looks?"

P.D.F.

*

"Middle age is when you suddenly find that your parents are old, your kids are grown up, and you haven't changed."

FRED SHOENBERG,
from *Middle Age Rage and other Male Indignities*

*

"OH COME ON - BEING 50'S NOT SO BAD, IT'S NOT GOOD BUT IT'S NOT SO BAD..."

"You know you're fifty when...
...you no longer recognize yourself in photographs."
PETER GRAY

*

THE OLDEST SWINGER...

"The aging swinger, flattering himself that he was still a ladies man, was flirting with a pretty waitress at his club. 'So tell me Darling, where have you been all my life?' 'Actually, Sir,' she smiled, 'for the first forty years of it, I wasn't even born.'"

S.L.P.

*

"He said, 'When you reach your 50s you must learn to grow old with grace.' I said, 'That's great! Bring her over and let's see what she looks like.'"

MIKE KNOWLES

*

"I may be 50, but every morning when I get up I feel like a 20-year-old. Unfortunately, there's never one around."

J.K.N.

*

"No one is ever old enough to know better."

HOLBROOK JACKSON

"WHOSE IS THIS WORK OF FICTION?"

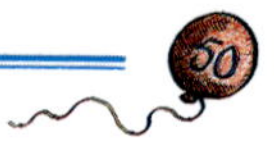

"THERE WAS ANOTHER WHICH SAID '50 - AND LOOKS IT' – BUT I DECIDED I'D BETTER NOT...."

"By the time you get to fifty people expect you to be mature, responsible, wise and dignified. This is the time to disillusion them."

PETER DUGDALE

*

"The older I grow the more I distrust the familiar doctrine that age brings wisdom."

H.L. MENCKEN

*

"Age is a very high price to pay for maturity."

TOM STOPPARD

*

"I was telling my son about the advantages of being over 50. 'As you get older,' I said, 'you get wiser.' He looked at me and replied, 'In that case you must be a genius.'"

ANGUS WALKER

*

Middle Age Spread!

"I'm at the age where food has taken the place of sex in my life. In fact, I've just had a mirror put over my kitchen table."

RODNEY DANGERFIELD

*

"In middle age it's helpful to remember a few basic diet rules:

1. If no one sees you eat it, it has no calories.

2. If you eat snacks quickly, or with your head in the fridge, they have no calories.

3. If you drink diet cola with a chocolate bar they cancel each other out."

N.J.R.

*

"Fifty is when you eat Death By Chocolate Cake with the nasty suspicion it might be just that..."

PAM BROWN

*

"O.K. - YOU'RE THE SAME WEIGHT AS YOU WERE AT 35.

YOU WERE A CHUBBY 35."

"NOW THERE'S SOMETHING YOU DIDN'T HAVE TO DO ON OUR FIRST HONEYMOON...."

YOU'RE GETTING "PAST IT"...

"...when you invite women to spend a moderately grubby weekend with you."

"...when making love turns you into a wild animal – a sloth."

"...when you don't need to chase women any more – I just hook them with my walking stick."

MIKE KNOWLES

"...when you look forward to a dull evening in."

"...when getting lucky means you've won the lottery."

"...when the spirit's willing – but the flesh is too damn tired."

PAM BROWN

*

A Total Physical Write-Off!

"Now I'm over 50 my doctor says I should go out and get more fresh air and exercise. I said, 'All right, I'll drive with the car window open.'"

ANGUS WALKER

"I'm getting to an age when I can only enjoy the last sport left. It is called hunting for your spectacles."

LORD GREY OF FALLODEN

*

"If you're pushing 50, that's exercise enough."

ANON

*

All In The Mind...

"At my age I don't care if my mind starts to wander – just as long as it comes back again."

MIKE KNOWLES

*

"You do not have to use your brains so much because they are a bit rusty."

KAREN EDWARDS, AGE 10

*

"You are fifty when you're still not sure about gadgets *everyone* else knows how to work."

PAM BROWN

*

"They say that when you're over 50 one of the first things to go is your...now what was I saying?"

ANGUS WALKER

*

"THAT'S FUNNY, I COULD HAVE SWORN IT WAS FRIDAY."

*

"Certain connections just seem to be beyond me at this age. For example, if someone calls me on the telephone and says, 'Can you meet me at the Seven-Eleven at eight?' I show up at the Five-and-Ten at nine."

BILL COSBY

*

"WHY DO PEOPLE SAY 'YOU'RE AS YOUNG AS YOU FEEL'? I'M ONLY 50 AND I FEEL LIKE THIS ALREADY?"

"The four stages of man are infancy, childhood, adolescence, and obsolescence."

ART LINKLETTER

*

"...you wake up one morning and there's a spot on your face, or the back of your hand, that you never saw before and you're sure it's cancer. Your eyesight has been getting steadily worse: brain tumor. A little gas: heart attack. Pretty soon you're showing symptoms of whatever ailment you saw on television the night before. I call it 'disease du jour.'"

FRED SHOENBERG,
from *Middle Age Rage and other Male Indignities*

*

"One of the saddest things of growing old is that you might have an illness that cannot be cured and the doctor might say, 'We are very sorry, very, very, but we are going to have to put you down.'"

ALEX STANGER, AGE 7

*

A Medical Condition

"Middle age is the time when a man is always thinking that in a week or two he will feel as good as ever."

DON MARQUIS

*

"Middle age: when you begin to exchange your emotions for symptoms."

IRVIN COBB

*

"FOR A FIFTY-YEAR-OLD, YOU'RE IN TERRIBLE SHAPE."

"NONSENSE. I DEMAND A SECOND OPINION."

"O.K. YOU'RE UGLY TOO."

Secrets Of Youth

"The secret to a long life is to stay busy, get plenty of exercise, and don't drink too much. Then again, don't drink too little."

HERMANN SMITH-JOHANNSON, AGE 103

*

The 2,000-Year-Old Man's Secrets Of Longevity

1. "Don't run for a bus – there'll always be another."
2. "Never, ever touch fried food."
3. "Stay out of a Ferrari or any other small Italian car."
4. "Eat fruit – a nectarine – or even a rotten plum is good."

MEL BROOKS

*

"I know a man who gave up smoking, drinking, sex, and rich food. He was healthy right up to the time he killed himself."

JOHNNY CARSON

*

The Body Beautiful

"You can only hold your stomach in for so many years."

BURT REYNOLDS

*

"It's hard to be devil-may-care
When there are pleats in your derriere"

JUDITH VIORST,
from *"To a Middle-Aged Friend Considering Adultery with a Younger Man"*

*

"You know you're getting older when a fortune-teller offers to read your face."

J.K.N.

*

"After thirty, a body has a mind of its own."

BETTE MIDLER

*

"I've got everything I always had. Only it's six inches lower."

GYPSY ROSE LEE

*

"WHY DON'T YOU DO SOMETHING USEFUL INSTEAD OF STRIDING ABOUT PRETENDING YOU HAVEN'T GOT A DOUBLE CHIN?"

"Old age can't get you if you keep moving."

PAM BROWN

*

"The best thing about being over the hill is that now you can have some fun and free-wheel down the other side."

ESTHER REES

*

"IT'S AMAZING WHAT PEOPLE WANT TO DO ON THEIR FIFTIETH BIRTHDAY..."

ACT YOUR AGE

"When you're over 50 you can still do all the things you did when you were 17... that's if you don't mind making a complete prat of yourself."

MIKE KNOWLES

*

"Boys will be boys, and so will a lot of middle-aged men."

ELBERT HUBBARD

*

"Time and trouble will tame an advanced young woman, but an advanced old woman is uncontrollable by any earthly force."

DOROTHY L. SAYERS

*

"Try to remember that, with the exception of your parents and your children, most people will consider you an adult."

FRED SHOENBERG,
from *Middle Age Rage and other Male Indignities*

*

"HE'S INTO DOING THINGS HE HASN'T DONE FOR A LONG TIME.

I LIVE IN HOPE...."